Meteor

Perspectives on an Asteroid Strike

Alex Woolf

Raintree

Chicago, Illinois

Edited by Andrew Farrow, James Benefield, and Claire Throp
Designed by Philippa Jenkins
Original illustrations © Capstone Global Library Ltd 2014
Picture research by Tracy Cummins
Originated by Capstone Global Library Ltd
Printed in China by RR Donnelley Asia

18 17 16 15 14
10 9 8 7 6 5 4 3 2 1

Library of Congress Cataloging-in-Publication Data

Woolf, Alex, 1964- author.
  Meteor : perspectives on asteroid strikes / Alex Woolf.
      pages cm—(Disaster dossiers)
  Includes bibliographical references and index.
  Summary: "What is it like to witness a meteor? This book looks at the Chelyabinsk Meteor and other asteroid strikes, using firsthand accounts to describe events and people's experiences, providing multiple perspectives from eyewitnesses, survivors, the emergency services, scientists, and the media"—Provided by publisher.
  ISBN 978-1-4846-0182-2 (hb)—ISBN 978-1-4846-0188-4 (pb) 1. Asteroids—Collisions with Earth—Juvenile literature. 2. Meteors—Juvenile literature. 3. Cheliabinsk (Russia)—Juvenile literature. I. Title.

QB651.W67 2015
523.5'1—dc23   2013040656

Acknowledgments
We would like to thank the following for permission to reproduce photographs: AP Photo p. 10 (Nadezhda Luchinina, E1.ru); Corbis pp. 9 (© Mike Agliolo), 14 (© Andrei Ladygin/ZUMA Press), 16 (© Reuters/Andrei Kuzmin), 19 (© Reuters/Andrei Romanov), 20 (© Heino Kalis/Reuters), 35 (© Ikon Images), 36 (© Bettmann), 40 (© Marcelo Hernandez/dpa); Getty Images pp. 6 (Michael Dunning), 12 top (Andrey Rudakov/Bloomberg), 25 (Alison Wright/National Geographic), 27 (Mandel Ngan/AFP), 31 (The Asahi Shimbun), 32 (Yuri Kadobnov/AFP), 38 (Nicholas Kamm/AFP), 46 (Erik Simonsen), 49 (Keith Johnson); Landov p. 18 (EPA/Sergei Ilnitsky); Nasa pp. 43 (JSC/Orbital Debris Photo Gallery), 44 (National Aeronautics and Space Administration); Newscom pp. 22 (Andrei Ladygin/ZUMA Press), 26 (Oleg Kargopolov/AFP/Getty Images), 29 (Travis Heying); Science Source p. 34 (Valeriy Melnikov); Wikimedia p. 12 bottom (Anthony Ivanoff).

Cover photograph of a factory building in Chelyabinsk damaged by the shock wave of the meteorite fall on February 16, 2013, reproduced with permission of Newscom (Jiang Kehong/Xinhua/Photoshot).

Every effort has been made to contact copyright holders of material reproduced in this book. Any omissions will be rectified in subsequent printings if notice is given to the publisher.

Contents

Some words are printed in bold, **like this**. You can find out
what they mean by looking in the glossary.

DOSSIER:
THE CHELYABINSK METEOR

On February 15, 2013, an 11,000-ton space rock, known as an asteroid, entered Earth's atmosphere over Russia. The asteroid was moving so fast that the air in front of it compressed (was squeezed). The friction of the air on the rock caused the rock to heat up and start to glow. Pretty soon it turned into a **meteor**—a dazzling fireball in the sky—that exploded some 14.5 miles (23.3 kilometers) above the province of Chelyabinsk in the southern Urals. The **shock wave** from this massive explosion was powerful enough to damage 7,200 buildings in six cities across the region, causing nearly 1,500 injuries. Fragments of **meteorite** fell to earth over a wide area. The Chelyabinsk meteor caused more damage, shock, and injury than any meteor impact in recorded history.

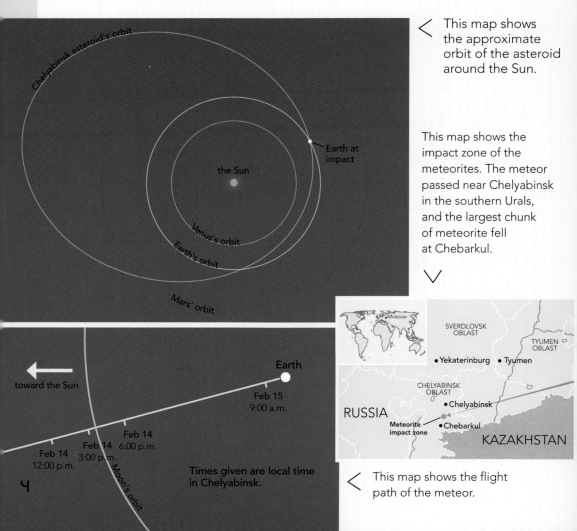

Chelyabinsk asteroid's orbit

Earth at impact

the Sun

Venus's orbit

Earth's orbit

Mars' orbit

< This map shows the approximate orbit of the asteroid around the Sun.

This map shows the impact zone of the meteorites. The meteor passed near Chelyabinsk in the southern Urals, and the largest chunk of meteorite fell at Chebarkul.

∨

Earth

toward the Sun ←

Feb 15
9:00 a.m.

Feb 14
6:00 p.m.

Feb 14
3:00 p.m.

Feb 14
12:00 p.m.

Moon's orbit

Times given are local time in Chelyabinsk.

Moscow

SVERDLOVSK OBLAST

TYUMEN OBLAST

• Yekaterinburg   • Tyumen

CHELYABINSK OBLAST

• Chelyabinsk

RUSSIA

Meteorite impact zone

• Chebarkul

KAZAKHSTAN

< This map shows the flight path of the meteor.

QUICK FACTS

TIME OF EVENT:	9:20 a.m. local time
SIZE OF ASTEROID:	56–66 feet (17–20 meters) diameter
SPEED OF TRAVEL:	Approx. 41,607 mph (66,960 km/h)
ENERGY OF EXPLOSION:	440 **kilotons** of **TNT** (20–30 times more powerful than the atomic bomb dropped on **Hiroshima** during World War II)

ASTEROID TIMELINE

4.5 BILLION YEARS AGO
The asteroid forms during the early solar system

3.5 BILLION YEARS AGO
It collides with another asteroid, which causes it to fracture and drift closer to Jupiter. The gravitational pull of Jupiter sends the asteroid into a different orbit, moving it toward the inner solar system.

10 MILLION YEARS AGO
It collides once more with another celestial object, making it loose and spongy and causing it to disintegrate fairly easily when it enters Earth's atmosphere

FOR MILLIONS OF YEARS UNTIL MID-FEB. 2013
The asteroid slowly spirals closer to Earth, with many near misses, until it is caught by Earth's gravity and accelerates toward it

Our Dangerous Skies

So what exactly was this object that appeared in the skies over Russia on February 15, 2013, and where did it come from? The object, before it exploded, was an asteroid. These are small, airless, rocky worlds in orbit around the Sun. They range from boulders of 3 feet (1 meter) to minor planets of 600 miles (950 kilometers) in diameter, and they number in the millions.

Asteroid belt

Most of the asteroids we know about are in the asteroid belt, a region of the solar system lying between the orbits of Mars and Jupiter. Astronomers believe asteroids are the rubble left over from the formation of the solar system. The **gravitational influence** of Jupiter prevented any planets from forming in that region. Instead, the small objects that were there collided with each other, fragmenting into the asteroids we see today.

When asteroids and meteoroids strike Earth's atmosphere, they grow very hot and start to glow. These are visible in the night sky. We call them meteors or shooting stars.

Near-Earth asteroids

Not all asteroids are in the asteroid belt. Around 10,000 of them have an orbit that brings them close to Earth. These are known as near-Earth asteroids (NEAs), and they are the ones that may, possibly, collide with our planet. If 10,000 sounds like an alarmingly high number, do not worry too much: space is extremely big, and the chances of an asteroid striking Earth are small.

Asteroids the size of the Chelyabinsk meteor hit us about once every 60 years. The reason we do not often hear about them is because most of Earth is made up of ocean and wilderness, and we simply do not notice the asteroids when they strike the planet. The other thing to remember is that Earth's atmosphere acts like a protective cushion, saving us from the worst effects of these impacts.

Monster asteroids

The atmosphere cannot protect us against really big asteroids, however. An asteroid with a 6.25-mile (10-kilometer) diameter, for example, could easily wipe out human civilization. But we would be incredibly unfortunate to witness something like that, as they only strike about once every 100 million years. (You can read about the consequences of a really big asteroid strike in the box below, and on pages 38–41.)

Chicxulub crater

We know for a fact that Earth has suffered many asteroid strikes in the past, because our planet still bears the scars of these impacts in the form of craters. One of the largest of these is the Chicxulub crater in Mexico. It is 111 miles (180 kilometers) wide, and the asteroid that formed it would have had a diameter of at least 6.2 miles (10 kilometers). By dating the rocks in the area, scientists have figured out that the asteroid struck around 65 million years ago. The force of the impact (equivalent to over 100 trillion tons of the explosive TNT) would have devastated Earth's climate for years, and many experts believe it caused the extinction of the dinosaurs.

Meteoroids

Although asteroids are relatively rare visitors, we get bombarded by smaller rocks, called **meteoroids** (under 3.3 feet, or 1 meter, in diameter), all the time. In fact, over 16,500 tons of meteoroids enter Earth's atmosphere every year, and they can be any size from a grain of dust to a boulder. Meteoroids are the shattered fragments of asteroids, **comets**, the Moon, or Mars following a collision with another **celestial body**.

This map shows the ten biggest impact craters on Earth.

	Name	Diameter in miles (kilometers)	Age (millions of years)
1	Vredefort	118 (190)	2,000
2	Chicxulub	106–186 (170–300)	65
3	Sudbury	81 (130)	1,800
4	Acraman	56 (90)	580
5	Woodleigh	25–75 (40–120)	364
6	Manicouagan	63 (100)	215
7	Morokweng	50 (80)	145
8	Kara	75 (120)	70.3
9	Popigai	63 (100)	35.7
10	Chesapeake Bay	53 (85)	35

Meteors

Most meteoroids never make it to Earth's surface. They enter Earth's atmosphere at tremendous speeds—up to 45 miles (72 kilometers) per second. When a body traveling at this speed passes through the atmosphere, it causes a great deal of friction. The meteoroid grows very hot and starts to glow. As it disintegrates, it forms a streak of light, which is visible in the night sky. We call these light trails shooting stars or meteors. Meteoroids that survive this violent passage through the atmosphere and reach Earth's surface are known as meteorites.

Bolides and superbolides

Asteroids, such as the one that exploded over Chelyabinsk, are bigger than meteoroids, so they burn brighter. Because they are so bright, they often go by the name of **bolides**, or fireballs. The brightest are known as **superbolides**. The Chelyabinsk meteor was a "superbolide."

Comets

Asteroids are not the only space objects threatening us. There are also comets—balls of ice, dust, and gas that orbit the Sun. When comets pass close to the Sun, their ice **sublimes** and they form spectacular dust-and-gas tails that can reach over 200 million miles (320 million kilometers) in length. A large comet could devastate Earth. However, such an event is even less likely than a large asteroid impact. Fewer than 100 near-Earth comets have been discovered. There is no proof that a comet has ever hit Earth, though some people think that a small one struck in 1908 (see pages 36–37).

The case of Ann Hodges

One of the first known cases of a meteorite injuring a human occurred on November 30, 1954, in Sylacauga, Alabama. Ann Hodges, a 31-year-old woman, was taking a nap on the couch in her living room when a grapefruit-sized meteorite crashed through the roof, bounced off the radio, and struck her on the side. She was badly bruised.

Big asteroid impacts are extremely rare. When they happen, the results are devastating for life on our planet.

The Chelyabinsk Meteor

The morning of Friday, February 15, 2013, began like any other in the city of Chelyabinsk in Russia. The sun rose at 9 a.m., its light gleaming on the peaks of the nearby Ural Mountains. People dressed warmly against the winter chill as they made their way to school or work. No one in the city could possibly know that a giant rock weighing more than the Eiffel Tower was speeding through the sky toward them at 50 times the speed of sound.

Fireball in the sky

At 9:20 a.m., people in Chelyabinsk noticed a burning fireball streaking across the sky to the south, heading from east to west. It was bright enough to cast moving shadows on the city streets. "I saw a flash in the window," said Maria Polyakova, head of reception at the Park-City Hotel. "I turned toward it and saw a burning cloud, which was surrounded by smoke and was going downward—it reminded me of what you see after an explosion." Valentina Nikolayeva, a teacher, described it as "an unreal light" that filled all the classrooms on one side of the school. "It was a light that never happens in life; it happens probably only in the end of the world."

A few people captured images of the fireball as it passed over the city of Chelyabinsk.

Airburst

The asteroid's enormous speed, combined with the shallow angle of its entry, generated so much heat and friction that it began to disintegrate. About 25 miles (40 kilometers) south of Chelyabinsk, at a height of 14.5 miles (23.3 kilometers), the meteor exploded. Around a fifth of the explosion's energy was released in the form of a bright flash of light lasting several seconds. Denis Kuznetsov, a historian, said that it shone "like 10 suns." The main explosion was followed by several smaller ones as the meteor continued to fragment.

Shock wave

The explosion occurred high enough above Earth to ensure that much of its energy was absorbed by the atmosphere. Nevertheless, when the shock wave hit Chelyabinsk and other nearby cities, it was still powerful enough to shatter windows and damage thousands of buildings. "My window smashed, I am all shaking! Everybody says that a plane crashed," tweeted local resident Katya Grechannikova.

The 1972 Great Daylight Fireball

On August 10, 1972, a fireball bright enough to be visible in daylight appeared in the skies above the western United States and Canada. The meteor did not plunge to Earth, but grazed its atmosphere, making its closest approach at 35 miles (58 kilometers) over Montana. The fireball sped northward at 8.8 miles (14.2 kilometers) per second, leaving the atmosphere over Alberta, Canada. During its 100-second flyby, the meteor was seen and photographed by many.

TIMELINE: CHELYABINSK ASTEROID

9:20:20 a.m.
The asteroid enters Earth's atmosphere over the Kazakhstan/Russia border.

9:20:33 a.m.
The asteroid (now a superbolide meteor) reaches its peak brightness. This is also the approximate time of the explosion.

9:22:40 a.m.
The explosion's shock wave reaches Chelyabinsk.

DOSSIER:
THE CITY OF CHELYABINSK

Chelyabinsk is a large city in Russia, approximately 950 miles (1,500 kilometers) east of Moscow. Built on the Miass River to the east of the Ural Mountains, the city is the center of government for its local **oblast**, or province, also called Chelyabinsk. The city's name comes from "Chelyaby," the name of an ancient village that had formerly stood on the site. In 1736, a Russian colonel founded a fortress there called Chelyaba, to protect surrounding trade routes from bandits. By 1787, the fortress had become the town of Chelyabinsk. The building of the Trans-Siberian Railroad in the 1890s helped turn Chelyabinsk into an important center of trade. During the era of the Soviet Union (USSR), Chelyabinsk experienced rapid industrial growth as a manufacturer of steel, tractors, tanks, and other weapons. It remains a major industrial center to this day.

Molten metal is poured into a cauldron aboard a railroad wagon at Chelyabinsk's metallurgical plant. The city is one of Russia's main centers of heavy industry.

Kirova Street is a pedestrian street in central Chelyabinsk. In addition to being an important industrial hub, Chelyabinsk is also a place of culture, with museums, theaters, and educational establishments.

POPULATION: 1.1 million

CLIMATE: January average temperature: 6.6°F (-14.1°C); July average temperature: 66.7°F (19.3°C); annual rainfall: 16.93 in. (430 mm)

TRANSPORTATION: Bus, tram, and trolley networks. A three-line subway network is due to open in 2017. The city is served by Chelyabinsk Airport.

TIME ZONE: YEKT (Yekaterinburg Time), eleven hours ahead of **Eastern Standard Time (EST)**

CHELYABINSK CITY TIMELINE

1736
Fortress of Chelyaba is founded

1890s
Construction of the Trans-Siberian Railroad turns Chelyabinsk into a major junction point and a gateway to the east

1897
Population reaches 20,000

1917
Population reaches 70,000

1930s
Chelyabinsk experiences rapid industrialization. The Chelyabinsk Tractor Plant and Metallurgical Plant are built.

1941
The Soviet leader Joseph Stalin moves military production east to avoid advancing German armies during World War II. This brings new factories and thousands of workers to Chelyabinsk. The city becomes known as Tankograd (Tank City). Chelyabinsk was virtually built from scratch during this time. Signs of the original town can be found in the city center.

13

Shock and confusion

The first reaction to the fireball, the chain of explosions, and the blast wave was shock. One witness said it seemed like an earthquake and thunder had struck at the same time. Another said the air smelled of gunpowder. "There was panic," said Sergey Hametov of Chelyabinsk. "People had no idea what was happening." Tyoma Chebalkin, a student, had a different impression: he reported that city-center traffic was at a standstill and everyone was trying to place calls, but he saw no signs of panic.

Many children were in school when the meteor struck. Classes stopped as students gathered at windows to watch the fireball streak across the morning sky. Was it a missile? A comet? A burning plane? They had to squint as the fireball suddenly blazed white—bright enough to cast shadows that slid swiftly across the ground. A series of explosions filled the air, followed by an eerie silence. Then, with astonishing force, the windows blew in.

The shock wave from the meteor strike smashed thousands of windows in Chelyabinsk.

Broken glass

Hundreds of video clips later posted online show ordinary mornings interrupted by a blinding flash and breaking windows. They show students and office workers thrown backward across rooms as the air is filled with shattered glass. The shock wave was powerful enough to smash not only windows, but also dishes, television screens, and computer monitors in hundreds of homes and offices.

Communications down

In the immediate aftermath of the meteor strike, the city lost its Internet and cell phone access. This might have been because of damage to cables or phone masts inflicted by the shock wave, or the system might have crashed because everyone was logging on or making calls at once. For whatever reason, no one could communicate, increasing the general sense of alarm.

Rumors

Without any news, people developed their own theories of what had just happened. Chelyabinsk resident Valya Kazakov said some elderly women in his neighborhood started crying out that the world was ending. Michael Garnett, the Canadian-born goalkeeper for the Traktor Chelyabinsk ice-hockey team, had some more down-to-earth theories. He thought it might have been "a natural gas leak or...a bomb or a missile or a plane crash." Alexander Yakovets, a local resident, thought it was a terrorist attack or military exercise. After an hour or so, the city's Internet coverage was restored, and news that it had been a meteor strike began filtering through the stunned population.

Bright flash and broken windows

At around 8 p.m. on November 26, 1919, a meteor was sighted traveling east above southern Michigan and northern Indiana. Witnesses said it resembled a brilliant illumination or a prolonged flash of lightning. In Athens, Michigan, the meteor was accompanied by thunder and heavy rain. The shock wave generated by the meteor's explosion broke windows and knocked out telephone communications and electrical supplies in several cities.

Injuries

Thousands of people gathered at windows to witness the event, not realizing they were in danger. The difference between the speed of light and sound meant that tens of seconds passed between the appearance of the flash and the **sonic boom** that blew the windows in (just as there is a delay between distant lightning and the sound of thunder). Russian television showed film of athletes at a city sports arena covered in blood after being showered by shards of glass from the arena's huge windows. Another video showed a long spear of glass slamming into the floor close to a factory worker.

No deaths were reported, but a total of 1,613 people asked for medical treatment, including 289 children. Sixty-nine of these stayed in the hospital, including 13 children. Apart from cuts from broken glass, there were cases of **concussions** and broken bones. Some fingers and toes were reportedly amputated. One 52-year-old woman suffered a spinal fracture and had to be airlifted to Moscow for treatment. Others suffered from **post-traumatic stress disorder.** Most of the victims were from Chelyabinsk and surrounding villages; around 130 came from the nearby town of Kopeysk.

Many Chelyabinsk residents had to receive treatment after being injured by flying glass.

Damage

The shock wave from the meteor's explosion damaged some 7,200 buildings in six cities across Chelyabinsk Oblast. These included 3,724 apartments, 671 educational institutions, 69 cultural facilities (museums, art galleries), 34 hospitals and clinics, 11 social centers, and 5 sports venues. The walls and roof of a zinc factory partially collapsed. However, most of the damage was to windows—around 2.15 million square feet (200,000 square meters) of glass was reportedly shattered. Many of the buildings were also left without gas because of damage to the energy supply **infrastructure**.

Official reactions

Within hours of the meteor strike, the regional government of Chelyabinsk Oblast announced that all schools were closing for the day and children were to be sent home. This was because of the broken windows, which would put children at risk from injury, as well as exposure to the cold weather. Offices in downtown Chelyabinsk were evacuated for similar reasons. In a message on the regional government's web site, residents were urged to stay at home if at all possible. Theater performances were canceled, as was an ice-hockey match featuring local side Traktor Chelyabinsk, after its stadium was damaged by the meteor.

Flying glass

Yekaterina Melikhova, an elementary school student, said she was in geography class when a bright light flashed outside.

"After the flash, nothing happened for about three minutes," she said. "Then we rushed outdoors...The door was made of glass, a shock wave made it hit us."

Yekaterina sustained cuts to her nose and upper lip.

Chelyabinsk resident Marat Lobkovsky said:

"I went to see what that flash in the sky was about. And then the window glass shattered, bouncing back on me. My beard was cut open, but not deep. They patched me up. It's okay now."

Operation Fortress

Shortly after the meteor strike, the Chelyabinsk authorities announced that police had been placed on high alert and had launched Operation Fortress to protect "vital infrastructure." They did not say what infrastructure or why it needed protecting. It might not have been clear at this early stage that they were dealing with a meteor—perhaps some officials suspected a terrorist attack. There are several nuclear power stations in the region, and one immediate concern was that these might have suffered damage, causing a **radiation** leak. But the authorities quickly confirmed that radiation levels in the region were normal.

The shock wave caused part of a wall, as well as 6,000 square feet (600 square meters) of roof, at Chelyabinsk's zinc factory to collapse. The incident caused a temporary rise in world zinc prices.

Meteorites

When the meteor exploded, it showered Chelyabinsk and the surrounding region with fragments of meteorite. These fell over an area of 39 square miles (100 square kilometers) across Chelyabinsk Oblast. Aleksandra Gerasimova, a retired milkmaid living in a village south of Chelyabinsk, reported being hit by a small meteorite that tore her coat and embedded itself in the inner lining.

One of the largest fragments discovered weighed 2.2 pounds (over 1 kilogram) and was found near Lake Chebarkul, 43 miles (70 kilometers) southwest of Chelyabinsk city. An even larger fragment broke through the ice covering the lake, creating a 26-foot (8-meter) diameter hole. A witness, who caught its landing on camera, saw it crash through the ice, sending up a jet of water. The fragment has now been retrieved. It measures almost 5 feet (1.5 meters) and weighs about 1,250 pounds (570 kilograms).

The first known meteorite injury

On April 28, 1927, at about 9 a.m., a five-year-old girl was playing in the garden of her house in the village of Aba, Japan, when she suddenly cried out. Her mother rushed over to her and found she had suffered head injuries in two places, and a small piece of stone had lodged in her collar. The stone, later confirmed as a meteorite, was hot to the touch. The girl was the first recorded human victim of a meteorite. Fortunately, she recovered after a few days.

DOSSIER:
ASTEROID 2012 DA14

Just 16 hours after the meteor struck Chelyabinsk, a larger asteroid narrowly missed Earth. It passed a mere 17,239 miles (27,743 kilometers) above the planet's surface, within the orbits of over 100 weather and **telecommunication satellites**, and it was visible through binoculars by observers in Australia, Asia, and eastern Europe. That is the closest approach of any known object of that size. Understandably, people wondered whether the two incidents were related. **NASA** scientists confirmed that they were not, because the asteroids approached Earth from different directions, had different orbits around the Sun, and had different compositions. It was just a massive cosmic coincidence!

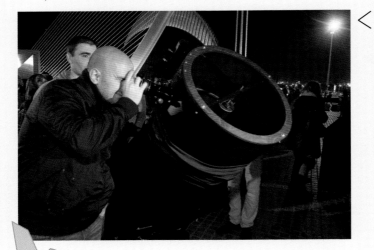

< A man in Valencia, Spain, uses a telescope to search for Asteroid 2012 DA14.

Boeing 747: 211 ft. (64 m) wingspan

2012 DA14 asteroid: approx 130 ft. (40 m) max. diameter

Chelyabinsk meteor: approx 56 ft. (17 m) diameter

House: 25 ft. (7.6 m) height

Person: 6 ft. (1.8 m) height

Here we can see the sizes of 2012 DA14 and the Chelyabinsk asteroid, compared to some more familiar things. >

QUICK FACTS

DISCOVERED BY: The Observatorio Astronómico de La Sagra, Granada, Spain

ORBITAL PERIOD: 368 days, which shortened to 317 days after its encounter with Earth

SHAPE AND SIZE: Elongated rock about 65 by 130 ft. (20 by 40 m)

SPEED: 17,400 mi. per hour (7.8 km per second)

RISK: Asteroids of this size are expected to impact Earth about once every 1,500 years and would produce an **airburst** equivalent to 2.1 **megatons** of TNT, enough to devastate a town or city

ASTEROID 2012 DA14 TIMELINE

FEBRUARY 23, 2012
The asteroid is discovered

JANUARY 9, 2013
The asteroid is re-observed by Las Camapanas **Observatory**, Chile

FEBRUARY 15, 2013
The date of its closest approach to Earth

FEBRUARY 15, 2046
Expected date of its next close approach to Earth

FEBRUARY 16, 2123
Expected date of its next close approach of similar distance to the 2013 encounter

The Emergency Services

We have looked at the experience of ordinary citizens caught up in the event, but how did the emergency services cope? The day after the meteor strike, an "emergency situation regime" was set up in the worst-affected towns and cities in Chelyabinsk Oblast: Chelyabinsk, Kopeysk, Yuzhnouralsk, Korkino, and Yemanzhelinsk. Around 24,000 emergency workers were mobilized from across the region, in order to sweep up broken glass, board up holes, and fit new windows. With temperatures falling below -4 degrees Fahrenheit (-20 degrees Celsius), repairs had to be done quickly.

Dealing with the injured

Meanwhile, hospitals handled the sudden influx of patients efficiently, thanks in part to the minor nature of most injuries. "The wounds that people have are mainly cuts and bruises, due to windows and window frames breaking and flying around," commented local surgeon Vladimir Basmannikov. Surgeon Sergey Vasilyev said that the blast broke a lot of windows in the hospital where he worked: "All surgeries were canceled and

The cleanup process begins in Chelyabinsk following the meteor strike. Within days of the incident, many stores had reopened for business.

we moved to the office where patients with broken glass wounds started to arrive…We have operated on 15 patients with multiple wounds of the face, head, hands, and body. Fortunately, there were several surgeons from different cities coming for **plastic surgery** training to our department so we could work in three operating rooms simultaneously."

Return to normality

Most of those injured made quick recoveries. A month after the meteor strike, 65 of the original 69 admitted to the hospital had returned home. Repairs to essential buildings were carried out quickly. By February 19, the region's schools and hospitals had all reopened. Over the next few days, the Emergency Situations Ministry announced that more than 175 tons of broken glass had been removed and almost 10,000 windows had been mended in 5,700 buildings. Some Chelyabinsk residents were taking no chances: in case of another meteor strike, they reinforced their window panes with rolls of sticky paper—a tip they learned from survivors of German air raids during World War II, more than 70 years earlier.

Contrasting reports

On March 5, the region's vice-governor, Sergei Komyakov, announced that 98 percent of the damage had been repaired and the emergency situation regime was over. The rest of the work will be completed "within five or ten days," he promised. However, according to a report by journalist Svend Buhl, by mid-April, less than 40 percent of the damage had been repaired—many homes and public buildings still lacked windows, and the city's airport and ice rink continued to bear the scars of the shock wave. Yet, claimed Buhl, the government's emergency relief fund had already been spent.

A new era

Chelyabinsk governor Mikhail Yurevich described February 15 as the city's second birthday (the city's official birthday is September 13, the date of its founding in 1736):

"If the meteor, which exploded above us, was just a little bigger, it's hard to imagine what could have happened to our towns and villages."

A mayor's perspective

Most people in a disaster zone will be concerned with saving themselves or their families. If they are doctors or rescue workers, their responsibilities will extend to helping other individuals affected. However, there are some people who have to think about the whole community. One is the mayor of a city. Have you ever thought about the difficult decisions people have to make when there is a disaster? Imagine you are the mayor of a city of 2 million people. Your city has just been hit by the shock wave of an exploding meteor. As mayor, it is your job to coordinate a response to this disaster.

You receive the following reports:

- Internet and phone networks are down in many parts of the city, meaning that any announcements made on your web site will not be received by a large proportion of the population.
- At least 150 people have been killed, and their bodies have been found lying in the streets or inside buildings.
- So far, around 3,000 people have called the national emergency phone line requesting ambulances or gone to emergency rooms of hospitals with injuries, mainly cuts from broken glass.
- Thousands more victims may still be stuck in their houses, unable to get through to emergency services because of the communication breakdown.
- Thousands of buildings across the city, including schools, hospitals, stores, offices, and apartment buildings, have suffered damage.
- Hundreds have been made homeless and will need emergency shelter, food, and medicine.
- There are at least five fires raging out of control in the city.
- There has been **looting** and violence in several streets where stores have been abandoned by their owners.

Your resources are limited:

- You have 100 ambulances at your disposal—not enough to deal with all the wounded in the city who need to be brought to a hospital.
- You have 40 fire engines—again, not enough to deal with all the fires.
- It will be 10 hours before more ambulances and fire engines are made available by other regional authorities.

- About 2,000 emergency workers are available for (a) search and rescue, (b) cleanup duties, and (c) repairs to the communications networks.
- About 8,000 police officers are available for helping to (a) maintain public order, (b) coordinate a citywide evacuation, and (c) organize emergency shelter.
- An additional 40,000 police and emergency workers can be brought in from other regional authorities over the next 24 hours.

It is up to you to make decisions about what actions to take and how to prioritize them.

Now that you have seen the disaster from the perspective of someone who has to make the decisions, do you think it is surprising that the authorities are so often criticized for their handling of disaster relief?

A major challenge facing emergency services after any natural disaster is dealing with refugees. Camps need to be established quickly, with adequate food, shelter, medical care, and sanitation, if a second humanitarian disaster is to be avoided.

Public Reaction

The meteor strike on Chelyabinsk was so sudden and unexpected that people's first reaction was, naturally, a mixture of panic and confusion. Gradually, however, as they learned the truth of what had happened, other perspectives and responses emerged, including humor, greed, excitement, pride, and suspicion.

Media response

As is often the case with natural disasters and other fast-breaking news stories, **media** outlets initially struggled to keep up with events. Rather than offering detailed reports that would be out of date almost as soon as they were published, news web sites put out short bulletins, continually updating the story with the latest information as it emerged. For example, the Russia Today (RT) network's web site published live updates every few minutes, as well as photos and video footage of the fireball. A lot of early coverage of the event focused on the remarkable coincidence of a meteor arriving on the same day as asteroid 2012 DA14 (see pages 20–21).

Russian Emergencies Minister Vladimir Puchkov (in red) is accompanied by journalists and photographers as he inspects the damage to a sports center in Chelyabinsk following the meteor strike.

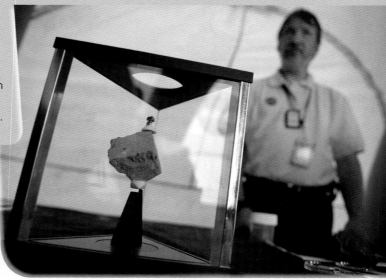

This meteorite fragment, on display at the White House, in Washington, D.C., came from Mars. It was ejected by Mars upon the impact of an asteroid and then landed on Earth.

Cashing in

Money-making instincts did not take long to surface. When the government announced that it would offer financial compensation to those who suffered damage in the meteor strike, it was reported that many locals deliberately broke their windows. They were expecting that the money they would receive from the government would be more than it cost them to replace the windows.

Within hours, "fragments of meteorite" were being offered for sale. "Selling meteorite that fell on Chelyabinsk!" a dealer named Vladimir announced on a popular Russian auction web site. Within days, there were offers of "Chelyabinsk meteorite fragments" ranging from $30 to $18,000, from sellers as far away as Portugal, Germany, Finland, and Latvia. The meteorite rush soon faded as public suspicions grew that most, if not all, of these stones were fake.

Breaking the news

News of the mysterious fireball and explosion initially spread via social media and local radio. Bizarrely, the first non-Russian news outlet to spread word was an ice hockey blog called *Russian Machine Never Breaks* based in Washington, D.C. It published a report about the explosion (it did not yet know the cause) at just after 11 p.m. Eastern Standard Time (EST), within an hour of the event, and before the Russian government had made any announcement. The blog's editors had been keeping a close eye on ice-hockey team Traktor Chelyabinsk, and a tweet from its goalkeeper, Michael Garnett, had alerted them. An official Russian announcement that "at least one meteorite has fallen in Chelyabinsk region" was made about an hour after the event and confirmed by the Associated Press on Saturday, February 16, at 12:21 a.m. EST.

Meteor products

One enterprising food manufacturer applied to the Russian patent agency to register a new range of meteorite-related food products. And local businessman Sergei Andreyev announced plans to launch a new perfume named Chebarkul Meteorite, which will feature "metallic and stony notes [scents]."

Fireball footage

Fascination with the event went global over the weekend of February 16–17, greatly helped by the dramatic footage of the fireball captured on "**dashcams**"—video cameras that Russians keep mounted on the dashboards of their cars. Within 15 hours of the event, dashcam videos of the meteor had been viewed millions of times on YouTube and other video-sharing web sites.

Meteorite hunters

In the days following the event, something akin to a "gold rush" gripped the people of Chelyabinsk, as thousands began combing the snow-covered countryside for meteorite fragments. Among those searching were the Belizkaya family. The meteor explosion had scared them at first—it cracked their ceiling and filled their home with oven soot. But they soon came to see it as something positive. On finding a meteorite fragment, Elena Belizkaya said, "This is such a memento of that event. We'll keep it at home for now, but if there's a chance to sell it, we'll sell some, of course!"

Jilin City meteor

On March 8, 1976, a meteor exploded over the outskirts of Jilin City in northern China. There was a giant boom followed by a series of quieter bangs lasting four or five minutes and heard by over a million people. Over 4 tons of meteorite fragments rained down over an area greater than 300 sq. mi. (800 sq. km). A survey team sent out by the Chinese Academy of Science collected hundreds of meteorites. They turned out to be **chondrites**—typical meteorites, made from an **accretion** of dust and grit from the early solar system. The heaviest, weighing 3,894 lbs. (1,766 kg), remains the largest chunk of chondrite ever found.

U.S. meteorite hunter Steve Arnold pulls a homemade metal detector across a wheat field near Haviland, Kansas. The device has helped Arnold discover a large meteorite buried in the ground.

Most meteorites were pea-sized, but some were as large as golf balls. They made mouse-hole-like craters in the snow. "It's like hunting or fishing," said one meteorite hunter. "When you see an animal, your heart starts to beat fast…This is the same— you see a tiny hole, try it, and here it is."

Conspiracy theories

In the wake of the fireball and explosion over Chelyabinsk, a Moscow daily newspaper polled its readers on what they thought it was. Barely half believed the official "meteor" story. The rest preferred to believe in a variety of other explanations given by some of Russia's more colorful characters.

Russian politician Vladimir Zhirinovsky claimed that the United States must have staged a secret weapons test over Chelyabinsk. "Nothing will ever fall [from space]," he told journalists. "If something falls, it's people doing that. People are the instigators of wars."

Was the meteor blown up?

A controversial yet influential Russian scientist, Yury Lavbin, claimed a UFO saved Chelyabinsk by destroying the meteor before it could land. His followers pointed to a dashcam video that, they claimed, shows this happening.

Another rumor was that local air defense units intercepted the meteor and blew it up to prevent it from falling on the city. The regional Emergencies Ministry had to deny this story.

The phantom text message

In the hours following the event, a spokesperson for the Urals regional Emergencies Ministry claimed a mass text message had been sent out, warning Chelyabinsk residents of the meteor. Locals denied ever receiving a message. The Emergencies Ministry later denied any message was sent, and the spokesperson was fired for spreading false information.

Environmental concerns

Some were more worried about the potential threat posed to the environment by the event. Vladimir Chuprov of Greenpeace Russia pointed out that the meteor struck just 60 miles (96 kilometers) southeast of the Mayak nuclear storage and disposal facility, which stores **weapons-grade plutonium** and **radioactive waste**. A similar distance to the northeast is the chemical weapons disposal facility at Shchuchye, which contains some 6,600 tons of **nerve agents**, including sarin and VX. If the explosion had occurred only a little farther east, these facilities might have been damaged, causing leaks of highly toxic substances.

Taking pride in the superbolide

Chelyabinsk is already making plans to exploit its newfound fame. The regional government has said it wants to be known as the Meteorite Capital of Russia. Various proposals have been put forward. These include hosting an annual "cosmic music and fireworks festival" or building a meteorite museum, a "cosmic water park," or a Disney-style theme park that re-creates the earth-shaking, window-shattering events of February 15. Others would like to brighten up Chelyabinsk city by painting space landscapes on its drab offices and blocks of apartment buildings. The mayor of Chebarkul, Andrei Orlov, plans to build a diving center at the lake so tourists can search for meteorites in its muddy bed.

Tours and exhibitions

Within weeks of the event, a Japanese tourist company was selling group tours to the city and the impact site, priced at $860 per person, and the city's history museum had installed a "Meteor Day" exhibit—a meteorite fragment surrounded by the front pages of newspapers from the day. The Museum of Local Lore planned an exhibition called "The Space Wanderer: Eyewitness Accounts," in which visitors could view photos, dashcam stills, and a film made shortly after the explosion.

"Space sent us a gift, and we need to make use of it. We need our own Eiffel Tower or Statue of Liberty."

Natalia Gritsay, head of the Chelyabinsk tourism department

"Nobody had heard about us and now all the world knows. We can earn some dividends [profit] on that. If there'll be a massive tourist inflow, we'll build more hotels."

Chelyabinsk Governor Mikhail Yurevich

This hole in the ice covering Chebarkul Lake marks the site where the largest fragment of meteorite struck. The lake is now a tourist destination.

Scientists at Work

A huge meteor strike observed and recorded by so many eyewitnesses is rare, so scientists were excited by the opportunity to study it. Using the data, they were able to figure out with surprising accuracy the nature of the superbolide, its mass, speed, and **trajectory**, and the energy it released when it exploded. In fact, most of the facts on pages 4–5 were known within a day or so of the event.

Calculating its speed and mass

The Chelyabinsk fireball was the most widely recorded meteor strike in history. Scientists studied huge amounts of time- and date-stamped video footage from dashcams, camera phones, and traffic cameras uploaded to the web. They were further helped by images of the shadows cast by street objects, marking the passage of the fireball.

The first video showed the asteroid at the moment it began to glow. The **gradient** of flight was about 20 degrees, and by calculating the angles from which the fireball was filmed, they could determine the height at which it broke up. It took about 10 seconds from entry to breakup, which told them its speed. Once they knew the speed, angle, and atmospheric heating of the superbolide, they could establish its mass.

By studying video footage, scientists were able to calculate the exact speed, mass, and trajectory of the meteor.

Origin of the meteor

Jorge Zuluaga and Ignacio Ferrin, astronomers from Colombia, used the video footage, as well as their knowledge of the impact site of the main fragment in Lake Chebarkul, to reconstruct the meteor's orbit around the Sun. It took an elliptical (oval-shaped) path beyond the orbit of Mars to well within Earth's orbit. They figured out that it was a near-Earth asteroid, probably originating from the asteroid belt.

Research by brothers Carlos and Raúl de la Fuente Marcos, from the Complutense University of Madrid, in Spain, suggests that the meteor may have been a fragment of a larger, 650-foot (200-meter) wide asteroid called 2011 EO. This asteroid regularly crosses Earth's orbit and is already listed as potentially hazardous. It is one of a cluster of around 20 asteroids, which are thought to be remains of an even bigger rock that broke up between 20,000 and 40,000 years ago.

Explosive energy

Peter Brown of London, Ontario, Canada, is a world expert at analyzing fireballs using infrasound—that is, sound waves below the range of human hearing. Infrasound reveals the energy of a fireball's explosion: the lower the frequency, the bigger the blast.

Humans cannot hear frequencies below 20 **Hertz**. The energy of the Chelyabinsk blast had a frequency of 0.03 Hertz, so low that Brown had to modify the software he was using. The shock wave was the most powerful ever recorded. In fact, a monitoring station in Greenland revealed that the sonic boom lapped Earth at least three times.

Infrasound monitoring stations

Peter Brown used readings taken from infrasound monitoring stations. There are 60 of these stations in 35 countries around the world. They detect nuclear explosions and ensure that countries follow the worldwide ban on **nuclear tests**. They are also used to measure things like meteor explosions.

Fragile rock

Scientists studying video of the fireball's final airborne seconds could immediately see clues about its composition. Pavel Spurny from the "fireball studies" team based at Ondrejov Observatory, in the Czech Republic, observed that it was "relatively fragile in comparison with other superbolides." Due to its possible collision around 10 million years ago (see page 5), the asteroid was described as "fairly loose and spongy," causing it to disintegrate quite easily when it entered Earth's atmosphere. Erik Galimov, director of the Institute of Geochemistry at the Russian Academy of Sciences, said the asteroid probably received multiple cracks as a result of the collision, which caused the meteor's powerful explosion.

Studying the meteorites

Russian scientists and volunteers were soon scouring the area around Chebarkul where most of the meteorites fell, in order to collect samples for analysis. Larry Taylor, director of the Planetary Geosciences Institute at the University of Tennessee, assumed the meteor must have been full of volatile material (substances that evaporate easily) to cause such an explosion. However, when the first meteorite samples were studied in the laboratory, it quickly became clear that it was a chondrite, a very common type of meteorite.

It was composed of about 90 percent silicate, a stony substance made up of minerals such as olivine, pyroxene, and troilite. The remainder consisted of metals, including zinc, iron, chrome, and aluminum. Professor Viktor Grokhovsky of the Institute of Physics and Technology at Ural Federal University, who led the expedition to collect the meteorites, says chondrites are the same age as the solar system— about 4.5 billion years old.

A researcher at the Vernadsky Institute in Moscow, Russia, uses a microscope to analyze meteorite fragments found at Cherbarkul.

Asteroids frequently collide with each other in space. Those that survive such impacts are often weakened by them. The Chelyabinsk meteor may have been weakened by an earlier impact.

Iron meteorites

We should be thankful that it was a chondrite. According to Phil McCausland, an earth science professor at the University of Western Ontario, if the meteor had been the much rarer "iron" type (made of 95 percent iron-nickel alloy), it would have made impact on the ground, rather than exploding in the atmosphere, due to its greater density and mass, causing far greater devastation. As it was, no more than 10 percent of the meteor's weight (around 1,100 tons) hit Earth's surface, according to Erik Galimov. The impact released barely a kiloton of energy, compared to 440 kilotons released by the atmospheric explosion.

The Pribram meteorite

On April 7, 1959, a meteor struck east of Pribram in the Czech Republic. The fireball exploded 8 miles (13 kilometers) above Earth. It was the first meteor to be tracked by several cameras. By studying the video recordings, scientists determined the meteor's orbit and landing place. Four pieces of meteorite were found, the largest weighing 9.8 pounds (4.4 kilograms).

As scientists began to take account of the events of February 15, 2013, many were struck by their similarity to the Tunguska event, which took place over 100 years earlier. In 1908, a massive explosion occurred near a remote river in Siberia, Russia, some 3,100 miles (5,000 kilometers) east of Chelyabinsk. Scientists believe the explosion was caused by an asteroid or comet entering Earth's atmosphere.

As with Chelyabinsk, theories soon began to circulate. Many Russians thought it was a sign that the end of the world was approaching; others believed it was caused by the crashing of an alien spacecraft. However, most experts believe that the Tunguska event was caused by the airburst of an asteroid or comet, 200–623 feet (60–190 meters) in diameter, 3–6 miles (5–10 kilometers) above Earth's surface.

This diagram shows the location and approximate flight path of the 1908 asteroid or comet.

>

Leonid Kulik led a series of expeditions to the site of the Tunguska event in the 1920s and 1930s. People took photographs to record the devastation. ∨

- Southern Swamp
- Chunya River
- explosion epicenter
- Podkamennaya Tunguska River
- Vanavara
- Chuna River
- estimated path of bolide
- edge of destroyed area
- 0   400 km
- 200 mls

EVENT:	The Tunguska event
LOCATION:	Near the Podkamennaya Tunguska River (now Krasnoyarsk Krai), Siberia, Russia
DATE AND TIME:	June 30, 1908, at approx. 7:14 a.m. local time
PROBABLE CAUSE:	Airburst from an asteroid or comet entering Earth's atmosphere
ESTIMATES OF THE BLAST ENERGY:	10–15 megatons of TNT (approx. 1,000 times more powerful than the atomic bomb dropped on Hiroshima, Japan, in 1945), making it the largest impact event in recorded history
EFFECTS:	Flattened approximately 80 million trees over an area of 830 sq. mi. (2,150 sq. km); broke windows hundreds of miles away; caused glowing sunsets in Asia and Europe over the following nights, probably due to dust particles thrown into the atmosphere

TUNGUSKA EVENT TIMELINE

1908
The Tunguska event happens

1921
Russian mineralogist Leonid Kulik visits the Podkamennaya Tunguska River basin and determines that the explosion was caused by a giant meteorite impact

1927–1937
Kulik leads several expeditions to the impact site and is shocked to find a huge area of trees scorched and stripped of branches—but no crater

1938
Kulik arranges an aerial survey of the area

1960s
The shape and extent of the zone of leveled forest is established. It resembles a huge butterfly shape of 43 by 34 miles (70 by 55 kilometers).

2010
An expedition by scientists from the Troitsk Innovation and Nuclear Research Institute (TRINITY) uses **ground-penetrating radar** to examine the Tunguska site. They find fragments of the celestial body. Analysis shows it was a huge piece of ice that shattered on impact, supporting a theory that a comet caused the explosion.

What Might Happen?

We have seen what happens when an asteroid the size of a small building, like the one that hit Chelyabinsk, strikes Earth. The disaster was serious, but manageable. Now let's speculate on what might happen if a larger asteroid struck—say, one 3,280 feet (1,000 meters) wide. Let's say it enters the atmosphere at an angle of 45 degrees and is moving at 11 miles (18 kilometers) per second.

Impact

In this case, the atmosphere is no barrier. Unlike smaller asteroids and meteoroids, a large asteroid is not slowed much by air friction, and it punches through the atmosphere as if it is hardly there. What *does* stop the asteroid is Earth itself. The collision creates a 60,000 megaton explosion. (The largest nuclear bomb ever built was less than 70 megatons, so it would be almost 1,000 times more powerful.)

With around 70 percent of Earth covered by ocean, the asteroid probably strikes water, but wherever it lands, the impact **vaporizes** the asteroid and forms a crater (or cavity in the ocean) approximately 12.5 miles (20 kilometers) wide.

The tsunami that hit Japan in March 2011 was triggered by an undersea earthquake. Tsunamis caused by an asteroid striking the ocean could cause even greater devastation.

Tsunamis and earthquakes

A land impact generates massive earthquakes that devastate nearby human settlements. An ocean landing creates **tsunamis**—enormous waves up to several miles high—that radiate outward in all directions from the impact zone. Traveling at around 185 miles (300 kilometers) per hour, these waves inflict massive destruction and flooding on every coastline.

The impact ejects thousands of tons of superhot matter into the air, including vaporized asteroid, material from Earth's crust, and—if it lands in the ocean—steam. It blasts this 62.5 miles (100 kilometers) into the sky, rising through a hole previously torn through the atmosphere by the asteroid as it fell (the asteroid is so big and fast, it pushes aside the air in front of it, creating a brief vacuum).

Impact winter

Some of this superhot ejected material falls back to Earth, starting mass fires around the globe. The rest spreads through the upper atmosphere, creating a blanket of dust around Earth thick enough to dim the sunlight. The fires send tons of smoke and soot into the air, making the sky even dimmer. The lack of sunlight reduces global temperatures and creates an "**impact winter**."

Scientists don't always agree on the aftereffects of a giant asteroid strike:

"The vast amount of debris thrown up from the explosion and the subsequent fires will create an 'asteroid winter' that might persist for several years, long enough for crop failures to lead to mass starvation."

From the web site of the Asteroid Terrestrial-impact Last Alert System (ATLAS) Project

"I feel that the threat of a dust-generated 'impact winter' is vastly overstated and that...[it] will not be anywhere near as severe... as some predict."

James A. Marusek, writing for the American Institute of Aeronautics and Astronautics, 2007

Global warming and UV radiation

After a few months, the dust settles, the sunlight brightens, and the impact winter comes to an end. However, the disaster for Earth's inhabitants is far from over: there follows a prolonged period of global warming—the **carbon dioxide** put into the atmosphere by the mass fires creates a **greenhouse effect**. With an ocean impact, there could be a further problem: the seawater vapor ejected into the upper atmosphere contains chemicals that destroy the **ozone layer**, which protects us from the Sun's **ultraviolet (UV)** radiation.

The effect on life

What is the effect of this speculative asteroid strike on humans, animals, and plant life? At first, there is chaos and panic in and around the impact zone. People living there experience earthquakes, tsunamis, floods, and fires. Casualties run into millions as the asteroid falls near large cities and hits an ocean near a heavily populated coastline.

Stores were raided by looters following an earthquake in Concepción, Chile, in February 2010. An asteroid impact could cause a similar breakdown in law and order, as people struggle to survive.

As the sky dims and the impact winter exerts its grip, the whole world starts to feel the effects of the asteroid strike. The reduction in sunlight slows down plant **photosynthesis**, threatening the entire food chain. Animals starve, and global famine looms. This leads to riots in city streets, the overthrow of governments, and a breakdown in law and order.

Assuming human civilization can withstand the impact winter, an even greater challenge lies ahead as Earth begins to heat up. We could face rising sea levels from melting ice sheets, flooding of coasts and lowland areas, and increasingly turbulent weather. Exposure to UV light can lead to sunburn, skin cancer, and damage to eyes and the **immune system**.

After impact

"The dust cloud would shield the Earth from ultraviolet light for an extended period ...After that, the ozone depletion would cause levels of ultraviolet radiation to at least double, about 600 days after impact."

Andrew Blaustein, professor of zoology at Oregon State University

How would we adapt?

Life would certainly have to change, but it would be possible for the human race to survive an asteroid impact on this scale, as long as people are willing to work together and make sacrifices. During the impact winter, there would be severe shortages of food and other essentials. In places where government authority survives, a system of rationing would need to be imposed, placing strict limits on how much each person is allowed to purchase. Elsewhere, the situation could turn ugly, with gangs fighting over what limited resources there are and many people forced to beg for food.

The period of global warming would probably last much longer, perhaps even decades, and it may be accompanied by an increase in UV radiation due to damage to the ozone layer. For both these reasons, humans would have to stay indoors during daylight hours and adopt a more **nocturnal** lifestyle. Until temperatures return to normal and the ozone layer repairs itself, we would have to find ways to grow food on indoor farms.

What Can We Do?

Our planet is just one of millions of rocks whizzing at tremendous speeds through space. It is inevitable that our rock will, from time to time, collide with other rocks. So what can we do?

Watching the skies

Most importantly, we can keep a constant lookout for rocks heading toward us. The more warning we get of a collision, the more time we will have to plan for it. We may even be able to launch a space mission to intercept the approaching rock (see page 47). The most dangerous rocks are those whose orbits bring them close to Earth, or near-Earth objects (NEOs). They include asteroids and comets. The type of NEO that poses the greatest threat is the near-Earth asteroid (NEA).

Since the 1990s, observatories around the world have been busy identifying NEAs. By July 2013, they had tracked 9,925 NEAs, 861 of which are 0.6 mile (1 kilometer) in diameter or larger. NEAs with orbits that could bring them close to Earth are called potentially hazardous asteroids (PHAs). According to NASA, there are currently 1,397 PHAs. The Minor Planet Center states that there are 1,409 PHAs.

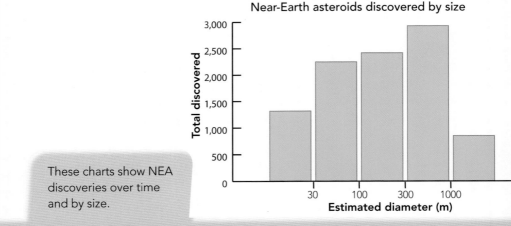

These charts show NEA discoveries over time and by size.

The Institute for Astronomy is in Maui, Hawaii. One of the telescopes situated here is Pan-STARRS (Panoramic Survey Telescope and Rapid Response System), used to track objects such as meteors and asteroids that could come close to Earth.

Why wasn't the Chelyabinsk meteor spotted?

One of the most disturbing aspects of the Chelyabinsk meteor was that it came without warning. With so many telescopes scanning the heavens, why did no one see it coming? One reason was its small size. More than 99 percent of the 9,925 NEAs spotted so far have been bigger than 328 feet (100 meters) in diameter, and the Chelyabinsk meteor was less than a fifth of that.

The asteroid also arrived during the daytime, and astronomical observations are more easily done at night. Furthermore, it approached from the direction of the Sun, and the Sun's glare prevented ground-based telescopes from seeing it.

Missed opportunity

Scientists differ in their views about whether the Chelyabinsk meteor could have been detected before it struck:

"It was impossible to detect it, because it was flying from the Sun. But if it was flying at night, our MASTER telescope network could have traced it."

Sergei Lamzin, deputy director of the Sternberg Astronomical Institute at Moscow State University

"It would be very faint and difficult to detect, not impossible, but difficult."

Paul Chodas, research scientist at the Near Earth Object Program Office at the Jet Propulsion Laboratory, Pasadena, California

What Have We Learned?

For many scientists and politicians, the Chelyabinsk meteor was a wake-up call: it was time to take a closer look at smaller NEAs. "I think that what surprised most people was the scale of the damage from a relatively small object and the fact that we didn't have any warning," said Hugh Lewis, a professor in aerospace engineering at the University of Southampton, in the United Kingdom.

In June 2013, NASA announced its new ambition: to track any space rock big enough to cause damage, including those less than 33 feet (10 meters) wide. NASA admitted it did not yet know how it would achieve this goal, but it invited individuals and private companies to come forward with suggestions.

Telescopes in space

One of the main problems is that NASA and other NEA-tracking organizations lack the resources to locate so many faint celestial bodies.

Space-based telescopes are likely to prove very useful in the hunt for the million or so smaller "city-busting" asteroids.

What they need are bigger telescopes, in more locations. Especially useful would be more telescopes in space. Earth-based telescopes suffer from a major disadvantage: sunlight masks their view of the heavens during the day, and at night the atmosphere distorts the light coming into their lenses (the same distortion that causes the stars to twinkle). By contrast: "A space-based asteroid hunter is…helpful because it can seek out space rocks at all hours of the day, as opposed to just at night," says Don Yeomans, manager of NASA's Near-Earth Object Program. The proposed space telescope Sentinel, which could launch in the next decade if successfully funded, would have the additional advantage of using **infrared** light, making it easier for astronomers to find objects that are too dark to be seen in visible light.

ATLAS

Even with the help of more space-based telescopes, a small NEA heading for Earth may still slip go undetected. As a backup, the University of Hawaii (with funding from NASA) is setting up a "final warning" program called the Asteroid Terrestrial-impact Last Alert System (ATLAS). The idea is to provide short-term warning of approaching NEAs. ATLAS will employ eight small telescopes that will scan the sky twice a night, more quickly but in less depth than regular NEA-hunting observatories. This will enable it to provide a three-week warning for a 390-foot (120-meter) diameter asteroid and a one-week warning for a 150-foot (45-meter) one. By calculating the trajectory, ATLAS could pinpoint the impact zone within about a mile or so, hopefully giving nearby areas enough time to evacuate residents.

Must do better

Not all experts are impressed with NASA's record in asteroid hunting:

"NASA has not even come close to finding and tracking the 1 million smaller asteroids that might only just wipe out a city, or perhaps collapse the world economy if they hit in the wrong place."

Ed Lu, former astronaut and CEO of the B612 Foundation, an organization building Sentinel, an NEA-hunting space telescope

The threat from bigger NEAs

Ideally, we would like more notice of an approaching asteroid than one to three weeks. With the bigger NEAs—those with diameters greater than about half a mile (1 kilometer)—this is certainly possible. In fact, NASA estimates that some 95 percent of these larger NEAs have been identified and tracked, and we can tell from their orbits if any are likely to collide with Earth. Currently, our biggest threat comes from Asteroid 1950 DA, which has a diameter of 0.7 mile (1.1 kilometers) and may possibly collide with Earth on March 16, 2880.

Intercepting the asteroid

So what do we do if a big asteroid is heading for Earth? According to experts, we could prevent the collision by intercepting the asteroid. "There are three ways to deflect a dangerous asteroid: the gentle pull, the swift kick, and by nuking it," says Alan Fitzsimmons, an astronomer at Queens University, in Belfast, Northern Ireland. The method chosen will depend on the asteroid's size, composition, orbit, and how much warning we get.

In the future, we may be able to use a spacecraft to deflect an asteroid from its collision course with Earth by firing a laser beam at it.

With plenty of warning, the "gentle pull" might be the best method. This would involve sending a very heavy spacecraft to hover close to the asteroid. The tiny gravitational pull created by the spacecraft should be enough, over a period of years, to shift the asteroid off its collision course. The "swift kick" entails a collision: a heavy spacecraft is flown into the asteroid, changing its orbit. A second "kick" may be needed if this does not work. The last and most desperate method is to "nuke" the asteroid. A nuclear bomb detonated near the asteroid would hopefully evaporate its surface layers and push it in the opposite direction. However, there is a risk that the asteroid may shatter, but continue in the same orbit: one big impact on Earth could be replaced by multiple smaller ones.

AIDA

The European Space Agency (ESA) is currently considering a mission to test the "swift kick" method of asteroid deflection. The mission is called Asteroid Impact and Deflection Assessment (AIDA), and the idea is to send up two spacecraft—one to collide with the asteroid, and the other to observe the results. The likely target is Didymos, a pair of asteroids in orbit around each other, and set for a close approach to Earth in 2022. Hitting the smaller of the two asteroids should, in theory, change its orbit around the larger one.

Practice makes perfect

"The first attempt to deflect an asteroid should not be when it counts for real, because there are no doubt many surprises in store as we learn how to manipulate asteroids."

Ed Lu, physicist and former
NASA astronaut

An international issue

Any impending collision would, of course, be a concern for the entire world—so decisions about how to deal with such a crisis need to involve every country. Plans are already in place to create a Space Mission Planning Advisory Group (SMPAG), made up of scientists from NASA, the ESA, and the world's other space agencies.

SMPAG (pronounced *same-page*) will meet annually to discuss new ideas for deflecting or destroying dangerous asteroids. If an asteroid is discovered heading for Earth, SMPAG will immediately meet to decide how best to intercept it. It will advise on how to build the intercepting spacecraft, using experts from around the world.

Emergency response

In case the mission to intercept the asteroid fails, governments will need to plan for the ensuing disaster when the asteroid hits. By plotting the asteroid's trajectory, scientists should be able to calculate the impact zone some days before, hopefully allowing enough time to evacuate any nearby towns and cities or coastal settlements bordering the ocean.

Government agencies, such as the Federal Emergency Management Agency (FEMA) in the United States, will need to act fast. They will have to use all forms of media to send out warnings and issue advice and instructions to the public. They should coordinate with local authorities, businesses, and **NGOs** so that everyone is ready to deal, as best they can, with the coming disaster. They will need to provide for search and rescue workers and equipment, evacuee transportation, emergency accommodation, food and medicine, and public security.

Catching an asteroid

In June 2013, NASA proposed an ambitious plan to capture an asteroid. It has selected three small asteroids, each about 30 feet (10 meters) wide. They plan to use an unmanned solar-powered spacecraft to drag one of the asteroids into orbit around the Moon. A manned mission could then be sent to it, which will hopefully help develop knowledge and skills that we can use to avoid future impacts.

Some countries will be better equipped than others at dealing with the crisis. But wherever the asteroid hits, the world should act together to deal with the consequences, and less-affected countries should offer as much aid as required to the stricken regions. After all, it could just as easily have landed on them.

Being prepared

The Chelyabinsk meteor served as a valuable reminder to us all of the ever-present threat from our skies. These events are thankfully rare, but we need to be ready for them. Just as governments in earthquake-prone or flood-prone areas have plans in place for dealing with these types of emergencies, so governments around the world should be prepared to deal with an impact event. Of course, the difference between asteroids and other types of natural disaster is that an asteroid can strike anywhere!

An emergency management team carries out a training exercise. We must hope there will not be a major asteroid impact in the foreseeable future, but if there is one, we need to be ready to deal with it.

Timeline

June 30, 1908	The Tunguska event: A comet or asteroid explodes over a remote part of Siberia
November 26, 1919	A meteor explodes above southern Michigan and northern Indiana, breaking windows and knocking out communications and electrical power in several cities
April 28, 1927	A meteorite injures a little girl in Aba, Japan – the first known meteorite injury
1947	The Minor Planet Center begins cataloging the orbits of near-Earth asteroids and comets
November 30, 1954	A meteorite injures Ann Hodges in Sylacauga, Alabama
April 7, 1959	A meteor strikes east of Příbram, Czech Republic. This leads to the first tracking of a meteor by several cameras, enabling scientists to plot its orbit and discover where it landed.
August 10, 1972	A meteor fireball is sighted during daylight above the western United States and Canada
March 8, 1976	A meteor explodes over the outskirts of Jilin City, northern China, showering the local area with chondrites (chunks of meteorite). One turns out to be the largest chondrite ever found.
1996	The Spaceguard System is established – a global network of observatories responsible for identifying and tracking near-Earth objects
October 6, 2008	For the first time, astronomers correctly predict an asteroid impact: 2008 TC3, which lands in Sudan on October 7
February 15, 2013	9:20:20 a.m. An asteroid enters Earth's atmosphere over the Kazakhstan/Russia border
February 15, 2013	9:20:33 a.m. The asteroid (now a superbolide meteor) reaches its peak brightness and explodes

February 15, 2013	9:22:40 a.m. The explosion's shock wave reaches Chelyabinsk
February 15, 2013	10:05 a.m. (approx.) (11:05 p.m. on February 14, EST) News breaks in Washington, D.C., of an explosion in Chelyabinsk
February 16, 2013	The first meteorite fragments go on sale on Russian Internet auction sites
February 16–17, 2013	"Meteor-mania" goes global, as dashcam videos of the meteor are uploaded onto YouTube and viewed millions of times
February 19, 2013	Affected schools and hospitals reopen
February 26, 2013	It is announced that Colombian astronomers have plotted the orbit of the Chelyabinsk meteor
March 5, 2013	The emergency situation is declared over
March 14, 2013	All but four people injured in the Chelyabinsk meteor strike have left hospitals
March 19, 2013	Russian scientists announce the weight and age of Chelyabinsk meteorite
March 21, 2013	Russian scientists discover a crater beneath Lake Chebarkul caused by a large meteorite fragment
June 2013	NASA invites experts to present ideas on capturing an asteroid

Glossary

accretion gradual buildup of additional layers

airburst explosion in the air

bolide large meteor that explodes in the atmosphere

carbon dioxide gas that is given off when fossil fuels such as coal, oil, and natural gas are burned. It is called a greenhouse gas because it traps heat from the Sun in Earth's atmosphere and adds to the greenhouse effect.

celestial body natural object visible in the sky

chondrite stony meteorite that contains small particles of iron and nickel

comet object with a core of ice and dust that, when near the Sun, forms a long tail of gas and dust particles

concussion temporary unconsciousness caused by a blow to the head

dashcam camera fitted to the dashboard of a car and used to record traffic incidents

Eastern Standard Time time zone that the eastern United States, Canada, and parts of eastern South America fall into

gradient angle of slope

gravitational influence force of attraction between masses, such as a planet and its moons

greenhouse effect trapping of the Sun's warmth by gases in Earth's atmosphere

ground-penetrating radar use of radar pulses to create an image of something below the ground's surface

Hertz unit of frequency, used for measuring sound waves

Hiroshima Japanese city that was the target of the world's first atomic bomb, dropped by U.S. forces on August 6, 1945, near the end of World War II

immune system organs and processes of the body that provide resistance to infection

impact winter prolonged period of cold weather caused by the impact of a large asteroid

infrared form of electromagnetic radiation just beyond the red end of the visible light spectrum

infrastructure buildings, roads, power supplies, and other basic structures and facilities needed for the operation of a society or business

kiloton unit of explosive power equivalent to 1,100 tons of an explosive material called TNT

looting stealing from a damaged or empty property

media term used to describe radio, television, newspapers, magazines, and the Internet

megaton unit of explosive power equivalent to 1.1 million tons of TNT (an explosive material)

meteor streak of light in the sky caused by a meteoroid entering the atmosphere

meteorite debris of a meteoroid that survives its passage through the atmosphere and hits Earth's surface

meteoroid small object of up to 3.3 feet (1 meter) in diameter that moves through the solar system

National Aeronautics and Space Administration (NASA) agency of the U.S. government responsible for the nation's civilian space program and for aeronautics and aerospace research

nerve agent one of a class of phosphorus-containing chemicals that are lethal to humans

nocturnal of the night

nongovernment organization (NGO) nonprofit organization that is not part of a national government and pursues a social or political goal. Examples include the United Nations, Red Cross, and Greenpeace.

nuclear test test carried out to determine the effectiveness of a nuclear weapon

oblast administrative division in Russia and other countries of the former Soviet Union, often translated as "area," "zone," "province," or "region"

observatory building that houses an astronomical telescope

ozone layer layer in Earth's atmosphere, around 9–22 miles (15–35 kilometers) from the surface, containing a high concentration of the gas ozone

photosynthesis process by which plants use sunlight to create energy from carbon dioxide and water

plastic surgery surgery involving the reconstruction or repair of parts of the body, either to treat injury or for cosmetic reasons

plutonium radioactive chemical element used as a fuel in nuclear reactors and as an explosive in nuclear weapons

post-traumatic stress disorder condition of mental and emotional stress resulting from injury or severe psychological shock

radiation energy and particles given out by something. Nuclear radiation is dangerous to living organisms, and so nuclear reactors are heavily shielded.

radioactive waste waste material containing harmful radiation that is a by-product of nuclear power generation

shock wave wave formed by the sudden compression (e.g. by an earthquake or explosion) of the substance through which the wave travels

sonic boom loud, explosive noise caused by the shock wave of an object traveling faster than the speed of sound

sublime change from solid to gas state without a liquid phase in between

superbolide extremely bright and large meteor that explodes in the atmosphere

telecommunication satellites artificial bodies placed in orbit around Earth for the purpose of communication

TNT (trinitrotoluene) highly explosive material

trajectory path followed by a moving object

tsunami huge wave caused by an earthquake, undersea landslide, asteroid impact, or other disturbance

ultraviolet (UV) form of electromagnetic radiation just beyond the violet end of the visible light spectrum. Ultraviolet radiation is part of sunlight, although the ozone layer prevents much of it from reaching Earth's surface.

vaporize convert into vapor

weapons-grade material that is suitable for making nuclear weapons

Find Out More

Nonfiction books

Atkinson, Stuart. *Comets, Asteroids, and Meteors* (Astronaut Travel Guides). Chicago: Raintree, 2013.

Owen, Ruth. *Asteroids and the Asteroid Belt* (Explore Outer Space). New York: Windmill, 2013.

Silverman, Buffy. *Exploring Dangers in Space: Asteroids, Space Junk, and More* (Searchlight Books: What's Amazing About Space). Minneapolis: Lerner, 2012.

Woolf, Alex. *An Asteroid Strike* (A World After). Chicago: Heinemann Library, 2014.

Fiction books

Johnstone, Michael. *Asteroid Strike* (Future Tense). New York: Franklin Watts, 2000.

Rose, Malcolm. *Asteroid* (Shades 2.0). New York: Ransom, 2013.

Movies

Cosmic Collisions: Our Explosive Universe (2010)
This documentary discusses near-Earth objects and the threat they pose.

Horizon: The Truth About Meteors (2013)
Produced in the wake of the Chelyabinsk meteor strike, this documentary explores what meteorites and asteroids are, where they come from, and the danger they pose.

NOVA: Meteor Strike (2013)
This is a documentary about the Chelyabinsk meteor strike.

Web sites

www.killerasteroids.org
On this web site, you can play a physics-based asteroid game, learn about how amateur astronomers are contributing to asteroid research, or carry out a simulated asteroid strike on any location in the world.

www.nasa.gov/centers/ames/about/overview.html
The NASA Ames Research Center looks at asteroid and comet impact hazards.

www.nasa.gov/mission_pages/WISE/news/wise20120516.html
This section of the official NASA web site gives up-to-date news about the search for near-Earth objects.

neo.jpl.nasa.gov/news/fireball_130301.html
This section of the NASA web site gives more information about the Chelyabinsk meteor.

www.purdue.edu/impactearth
This site is another asteroid impact calculator in which you enter information about an imaginary strike and learn about its destructive effects.

More topics to research

1. Research and write your own "disaster dossier" on a meteor strike not mentioned in this book. Examples could include the fireball witnessed above New York City on November 15, 1859; the meteorite shower near Helsinki, Finland, on March 12, 1899; or the so-called "Brazilian Tunguska event" near the Curuçá River area, Amazonas, Brazil, of August 13, 1930.

2. Imagine you are the head of an emergency management agency in a city and you have just been informed that a 60-foot (20-meter) wide asteroid is heading toward your region, due to strike in around 20 hours. What actions could you take now to minimize loss of life and long-term damage to your city?

3. Take a look at the down2EARTH Impact Calculator at education.down2earth.eu/impact_calculator.
   Select values to describe an asteroid strike of your choice, then click "submit" to discover the consequences. Try entering different values and see what difference it makes. What factors cause the most damage as you increase them: asteroid diameter, trajectory angle, object velocity, or projectile density?

Index